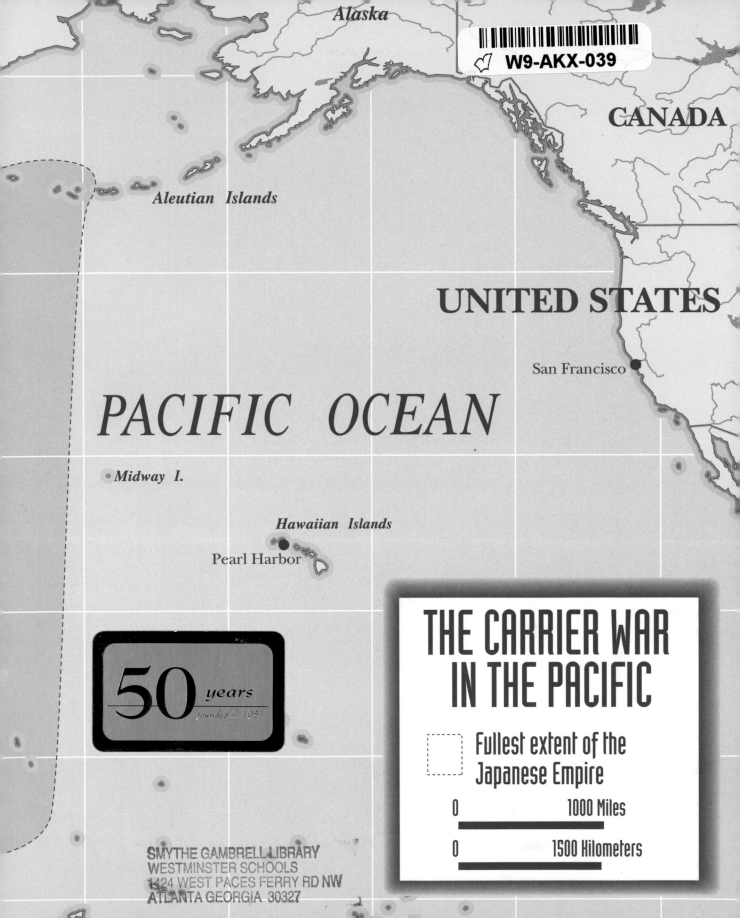

Alaska

CANADA

Aleutian Islands

UNITED STATES

PACIFIC OCEAN

San Francisco

• Midway I.

Hawaiian Islands

Pearl Harbor

THE CARRIER WAR
IN THE PACIFIC

Fullest extent of the
Japanese Empire

0   1000 Miles

0   1500 Kilometers

Tom McGowen

CARRIER WAR

AIRCRAFT CARRIERS IN WORLD WAR II

2002 David Boyd

Cover photograph courtesy of Hulton Getty/Liaison Agency

Photographs courtesy of San Diego Aerospace Museum: pp. 4, 7, 9, 12, 23, 24, 25, 29, 35, 40, 42, 43, 44; U. S. Naval Historical Foundation Center: p. 11; Hulton Getty/Liaison Agency: pp. 14, 17, 19, 20, 26, 31, 36, 48, 55; Archive Photos: pp. 39, 58, 60; Admiral Nimitz National Museum of the Pacific War, Fredericksburg, Texas: p. 63

Library of Congress Cataloging-in-Publication Data
McGowen, Tom.
Carrier war : aircraft carriers in World War II / Tom McGowen.
p. cm. — (Military might)
Includes bibliographical references and index.
ISBN 0-7613-1808-9
1. Aircraft carriers—History—20th century—Juvenile literature. 2. World War, 1939-
–1945—Naval operations, American—Juvenile literature. 3. World War, 1939–1945—Naval operations, Japanese—Juvenile literature. 4. World War, 1939–1945—Naval operations, British—Juvenile literature. 5. World War, 1939–1945—Aerial operations, American—Juvenile literature. 6. Aerial operations, Japanese—Juvenile literature. 7. Aerial operations, British—Juvenile literature. [1. Aircraft carriers—History. 2. World War, 1939–1945—Naval operations. 3. World War, 1939–1945—Aerial operations.] I. Title. II. Series.
D770 .M35 2001
940.54'5—dc21 00-042303

Published by Twenty-First Century Books
A Division of The Millbrook Press, Inc.
2 Old New Milford Road
Brookfield, Connecticut 06804
www.millbrookpress.com

Contents

Chapter 1

A NEW WEAPON FOR SEA WARFARE

As the twentieth century began, the main warships of the world's navies were battleships, cruisers, and battle cruisers—huge, heavily armored vessels bristling with giant guns. These were the weapons of sea power, and the most powerful of them were the battleships, the main fighting ships of every navy. They were considered the major weapon of sea battle.

But soon after the invention of the airplane, in 1903, some naval officers began to think about the possibility of a new, special kind of warship—a warship that carried airplanes instead of guns.

Warships then had no such thing as radar, and the only way of locating enemy ships was to *see* them, by peering through binoculars. But with even the highest power binoculars, it was possible to see only a few miles distant. A ship with planes that could take off from and land on it, would provide a fleet of warships with a number of far-seeing "eyes." The planes could fly

The first airplane used by the U.S. Navy was this Curtiss A-1.

5

far from their ships in all directions, and their pilots could scan the sea for enormous distances, looking for enemy ships. Being able to discover the location and number of an enemy force many miles away would be a tremendous advantage for a fleet.

However, there were some questions to be answered. Could an airplane even take off from a ship, or would it simply fall into the water? Could an airplane make a landing on such a narrow space as the deck of a ship?

There were also problems about the *structure* of a ship to carry airplanes. For planes to take off, a long flat area with nothing in the way was essential. But there were lots of things in the way on a ship's deck. All navy ships were fueled by coal, and they had smokestacks, which stuck straight up from the deck. Every ship had a bridge, an enclosed structure from which the ship is steered and controlled, and the bridge, too, stuck up from the deck. Everything sticking up above the deck of a ship is known as the *superstructure*, and as long as there was superstructure obstructing a ship's deck, there was just no room for planes to take off.

Navies began trying to answer the questions and solve the problems. On a bright day in November 1910, an American warship lay at anchor in a harbor in Virginia. It had an odd look, because a sloping platform 83 feet long (about 25 meters) had been erected on the front deck, leading to the very edge of the ship's front end. At the back end of the platform sat an airplane. Its upper and lower wings and its rudder and tail were covered with cloth, and the body was simply an open framework of wooden struts, but at that time the plane was a marvel of up-to-the-minute technology.

At a signal the anchor was pulled up, and the ship began to move to get the wind behind it. A man clambered into the aircraft, seating himself in the open framework between the wings, where the controls were located. He was a civilian pilot named Eugene Ely, and the plane belonged to a company he worked

Eugene Ely taking off from the deck of the USS Pennsylvania
*in San Francisco Bay in January 1911, two months after his
successful flight in Virginia*

for, because the U.S. Navy had no airplane pilots nor any airplanes. Ely turned on the engine, and the propeller blades
began to whirl. At the top speed the plane could manage, he
took it rushing down the sloping platform. Reaching the platform's end, it sailed off the end of the ship and instantly
dropped, its undercarriage actually touching the water for a
moment. But it was moving fast enough to stay in the air. Ely
guided it upward until it was well above the ship.

The main question—Could a plane take off from a ship?—had been answered.

However, taking off from the deck of a ship seemed a lot easier than landing on one, because an airplane had to be able to roll a long way before it came to a stop. It could easily roll right off the end of a ship's deck! Two months after his successful takeoff, Ely tried a landing on the deck of a warship moored in San Francisco Bay. A platform 102 feet long and 32 feet wide (about 30 by 10 meters) had been erected on its deck, and stretched across the width and fastened in place were 22 ropes a number of feet apart from one another. From the bottom of Ely's plane hung three large hooks, facing forward. Flying to the rear end of the ship, Ely slowly brought his plane down until it was rolling along the platform. When the plane reached the twelfth rope, the hooks caught on it. The rope stretched but didn't break or pull loose, and the plane was brought to a quick stop.

The first two steps toward creating a totally new kind of ship—an aircraft carrier—had been taken. An airplane could both take off from and land on a ship.

Now the problems involving the ship itself had to be solved. Obviously, erecting a platform on a ship's deck was not a good answer. In July 1914 the British Navy tried to solve the problem in a different way. Seaplanes—planes with floats instead of wheels, which could take off and land on water—had recently been invented. The British took an old warship, *Hermes*, and built a canvas hangar on it that held three seaplanes. A crane was also built onto the ship, and when a plane was to make a flight, it was lowered into the water by the crane, and it took off. Finishing its flight, it came down in the water near the ship and was hoisted back aboard by the crane.

In 1914, World War I broke out in Europe. The *Hermes* was sunk by a German submarine, but the British turned several other ships into seaplane carriers. They also got the idea of

*Eugene Ely making the first successful carrier landing
in January 1911 on the deck of the USS* Pennsylvania

using carrier planes for something other than scouting, and
invented the first kind of torpedo that could be dropped from
an airplane. A British carrier plane was the first airplane to sink
a ship with a torpedo.

However, it was soon realized that seaplanes really couldn't
do as well as planes that could take off from land. They weren't
as fast, and they couldn't maneuver as well. The British Navy

began experimenting with small planes that could get airborne quickly, and with platforms on various kinds of ships, but it became clear that the deck of an ordinary ship with a super-structure just wouldn't work. What was needed was a flat deck with nothing sticking up from it. The only answer was to construct a special sort of ship with that kind of deck.

By the war's end, the British had built the first workable air-craft carrier, which was christened the *Argus*. The problem of the superstructure had been solved. No smokestacks stuck up from the deck, because the smokestacks were lying flat *underneath* the deck. The bridge had been replaced by a number of compartments also under the deck. Thus, the *Argus*'s deck was completely flat, and the ship was soon nicknamed "the flatiron," because she resembled a laundry iron of those days. The *Argus* carried 15 airplanes.

The war ended before the *Argus* was ever used in combat, but Great Britain, the United States, and the Empire of Japan were impressed enough by the possibilities of aircraft carriers that they all began to build some. The Japanese Navy launched its first carrier, the *Hosho*, in 1921. She had a deck 500 feet long (about 150 meters) and carried 21 airplanes. America's first car-rier was the *Langley*, which went into service in 1922. She was 542 feet long (about 160 meters) and could carry 36 airplanes.

By the mid-1930s, aircraft carriers had become fairly stan-dardized. They were, literally, floating airfields. The top deck, known as the flight deck, was the runway, where planes took off and landed. It was flat, clear, and generally from about 600 to 900 feet long (180 to 270 meters) and 60 to 80 feet wide (18 to 24 meters). A small narrow superstructure containing the bridge, and sometimes a single large smokestack, was perched way off to one side at the edge of the deck, and was known as "the island."

The HMS Argus. *The camouflage paint was intended to disguise the ship's direction.*

Below the flight deck was the hangar deck, where planes were stored, repaired, and armed for battle. To provide more room for storage, the wings of carrier planes folded upward, so the planes could be pushed closer together. To get planes from the hangar deck to the flight deck there was a huge section (sometimes two) of the flight deck that was actually an elevator that could be lowered and raised. It was lowered, and planes were put on it, lifted up, and pushed into place on the flight deck while the elevator went back down for more. When all planes were in position, the elevators were flush with the flight deck, becoming part of the smooth runway needed for takeoff.

The USS Langley

There were three kinds of carrier airplanes. Torpedo bombers carried a single large torpedo that was dropped into the water as the plane flew low over the water straight at an enemy ship. Dive-bombers were armed with one large or two small bombs that were dropped on a ship as the plane dived almost straight down at it. Fighter planes either flew above a carrier to protect it from enemy bombers, or went with bombers to protect them against enemy fighters. Most British carriers used only torpedo planes and fighters.

These were the kinds of carriers and carrier planes in the navies of the United States, Great Britain, and the Empire of Japan, when war broke out again in Europe in 1939. Germany invaded Poland, and immediately France and Great Britain declared war on Germany. World War II was under way.

Chapter 2

THE U.S. BASE AT PEARL HARBOR

War was also going on in Asia. Since 1931, the Empire of Japan had been slowly conquering its big neighbor, China. The United States was trying to help China, mainly by preventing Japan from getting oil, steel, and other things it needed to keep its conquest going. This had made relations between the United States and Japan rather strained. Some people felt sure the two nations would eventually go to war. And late in 1941 war did break out between the United States and Japan. It was to be a war in which aircraft carriers, the new weapon of sea warfare, would play a major role.

Throughout the Pacific Ocean are many thousands of islands. Some are no more than a few miles wide, but some are thousands of square miles in size, with mountains, forests, and rivers. In 1941 the United States, Japan, Great Britain, France, and the Netherlands all possessed a number of these islands that they used as military and naval bases, with docks for warships, airfields for planes, living quarters for troops, storage areas for huge amounts of supplies, fuel, and ammunition, and

Pearl Harbor, Hawaii: the Japanese attack has begun

repair facilities for ships and planes. It was known that if war ever broke out in the Pacific, there would be fighting for possession of these bases.

The war in the Pacific began at an American base on the island of Oahu, Hawaii. On the southern coast of Oahu, a narrow channel of water leads from the Pacific Ocean into Pearl Harbor, a 10-square-mile (26-square-kilometer) harbor with a small island, Ford Island, in the middle. Pearl Harbor and the scores of buildings clustered around it for several miles formed the largest U.S. Navy base in the Pacific Ocean. As dawn was breaking over Oahu on the morning of December 7, 1941, 96 ships of the U.S. Navy's Pacific Fleet lay at anchor or tied up at docks in Pearl Harbor.

Arranged in a row stretching along the side of Ford Island were seven battleships, with an eighth some distance beyond, in drydock for repairs. American battleships were named for states, and those in the row were the *Arizona, California, Maryland, Nevada, Oklahoma, Tennessee,* and *West Virginia.* The battleship in drydock was the *Pennsylvania.*

Eight cruisers were also moored at Pearl Harbor. Cruisers were basically just lighter battleships—about the same size as a battleship but with less armor and smaller guns. There were also 30 destroyers and a number of other small ships at Pearl Harbor. A destroyer was a 340- to 380-foot (102- to 114-meter) unarmored ship that could move fast and change direction quickly, used mainly for protecting bigger and slower ships, especially against submarines.

One of the ships anchored in Pearl Harbor was not a fighting ship, but she was a ship that was essential to the Navy. She was the *Neosho,* the kind of ship called an oiler, or tanker. All the warships of World War II ran on oil, and every navy had ships called oilers, which were tankers filled with huge amounts of oil that could be pumped into the fuel tanks of warships. A fleet of ships that would have to be out at sea for any length of time had to have several oilers with it, and the need to stop and

The launching of the HMS Illustrious, *the largest ship ever built for the Royal Navy*

refuel the fleet from time to time often meant the difference between catching up to an enemy force or getting caught by an enemy force!

Only Great Britain, Japan, and the United States had aircraft carriers in their navies in the first few years of World War II. However, the men who commanded these navies at the beginning of the war really didn't quite know how to best use an aircraft carrier. In fact, many high-ranking naval officers felt that aircraft carriers really weren't of much use. Carriers had little armor and no guns other than anti-aircraft guns for defense, so they were generally regarded as an "eggshell"—a lightly armored ship that could be easily destroyed, as compared to a heavily armored battleship. They were thought of as strictly a "support" weapon, or helper, for battleships. They used their bombers to attack enemy ships their battleships were fighting, or they used their fighter planes to protect their battleships from enemy planes. They were generally used this way early in World War II.

However, in 1940, an aircraft carrier had shown what carriers could do by themselves without any help from battleships. Planes from the British carrier *Illustrious* flew to the naval base of Taranto on the coast of Italy and made an attack on the main Italian fleet anchored there. The planes heavily damaged three battleships, putting them out of action for a long time. A few high-ranking naval officers, one of them a Japanese admiral named Isoroku Yamamoto, began to realize that perhaps aircraft carriers could be a far more dangerous weapon than was generally believed.

The United States Navy had seven aircraft carriers at the beginning of World War II. Three were named for Revolutionary War battles—*Lexington*, *Yorktown*, and *Saratoga*. Two were named for flying stinging insects—*Wasp* and *Hornet*. One was named *Enterprise*, a word meaning a bold undertaking. One was named *Ranger*. None of America's aircraft carriers were at Pearl Harbor that December morning in 1941, and that

Admiral Isoroku Yamamoto

would turn out to be one of the greatest pieces of luck America had during the war that was about to begin.

As things started to stir aboard the ships at Pearl Harbor that morning, something was happening a few hundred miles away, out at sea, that was going to shatter the peace of the Sunday morning and pull America violently into World War II.

Chapter 3

OPERATION Z

Some 275 miles (455 kilometers) north of Pearl Harbor, the first rays of morning sunlight were gleaming off the gray sides of a fleet of 23 warships of the Empire of Japan.

This fleet had been assembled with as much secrecy as possible, and had sailed toward Hawaii on a great curving course far out of regular ship lanes. If a ship of another country had been encountered, it would have been sunk by gunfire and torpedoes, so that it couldn't report what it had seen. The fleet's destination and its purpose was a gigantic secret that had to be kept at any cost.

Two of the vessels were battleships. There were three cruisers and eight destroyers, three bulky oilers, and a supply ship. But the main ships of this fleet were six big aircraft carriers, carrying a total of 360 airplanes. The other ships were just guardians and suppliers. The six carriers were the striking force that was going to carry out the plan, known as Operation Z, that had been worked out by the Japanese high command. That

*Japanese pilots stride toward their bombers on board
a Japanese carrier—destination Pearl Harbor*

plan called for a surprise air attack on the American warships in Pearl Harbor.

The Japanese intended to attack without declaring war. By doing such a thing they were ignoring a long-standing rule of warfare. Many Japanese military leaders were actually against this, but the top leaders were determined that it had to be done. They had decided there was no choice but war. If the United States was not going to sell Japan the oil, steel, and other things it needed, Japan would have to get them elsewhere. The only way to do that was by conquering the parts of Asia where those things could be obtained. This could not have been done a few years earlier, because most of those places were colonies of France, the Netherlands, and Great Britain. But now, France and the Netherlands had been conquered by Germany, and Great Britain was fighting for its life. The colonies were on their own, with no chance of help from their mother countries if Japan moved against them.

However, Japan's leaders knew that if they began a war of conquest they would face certain war with the United States. They realized that over a long period of time American industry would be able to produce far more warships and weapons than Japan could, and if the war were to last more than two years, Japan would eventually be defeated. So, they had to find a sure way of winning the war quickly.

It was Admiral Isoroku Yamamoto, commander in chief of the Japanese navy, who came up with a plan to do that. He felt sure that if Americans were convinced they had no chance, they would make peace and let Japan do as it wished in the Pacific region. So he worked out a plan to wipe out the main power of the United States Pacific Fleet, its battleships. He believed that if all or most of them could be destroyed, the American navy would become powerless against the navy of Japan, with its eleven battleships. He also believed that the way to destroy the American ships was by means of an attack of airplanes from aircraft carriers, as the British had done at Taranto. Thus, the main purpose of the air strike about to be launched toward Hawaii was to do the most damage possible to the eight American battleships sitting in a row at Pearl Harbor. Only Japan's possession of aircraft carriers made such an attack possible; it was from the six carriers that the planes making the attack would be launched.

Japanese aircraft carriers had dramatic, poetic names, in keeping with the culture and legends of Japan. The carrier *Akagi*'s name meant Red Castle, the *Kaga* was Increased Joy, the *Soryu* was Green Dragon, the *Hiryu* was Flying Dragon, the *Shokaku* was Soaring Crane, the *Zuikaku*, Happy Crane. But

A Mitsubishi A6M "Zero"

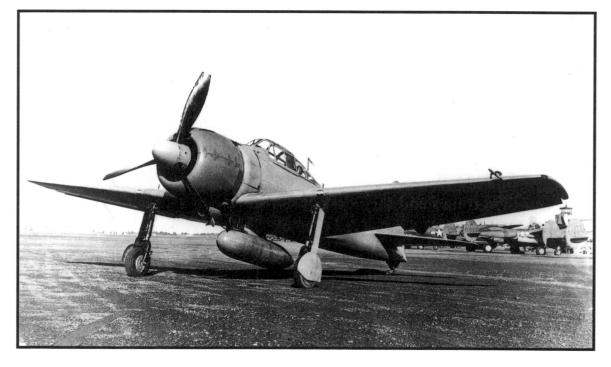

A Nakajima B5N "Kate"

there was nothing poetic about the carriers as their planes were prepared for launch. All was businesslike and fiercely eager!

On each ship the fighter planes were placed to leave first. These were the Mitsubishi A6M Reisen fighters that became known to Americans as Zeros, or "Zekes." Their usual job was to shoot down any enemy plane that came into their gunsights, but today they would mainly be strafing—shooting up targets on the ground and the decks of ships.

After them were the Nakajima B5N bombers, known as attack bombers in the Japanese navy, and called "Kates" by Americans. Each carried a one-ton bomb. Next came the Aichi D3A1 dive-bombers, known to Americans as "Vals." They carried a 550-pound (250–kilogram) bomb or two 132-pound (60-kilogram) bombs. Last to take off would be another group of "Kates" armed to be torpedo bombers, with a 1,764-pound torpedo each.

The pilots and crew members of all the planes were strapped into their seats, their plane engines roaring. The carriers turned into the wind and increased their speed, so that the push of the wind would help the planes get airborne. All six carriers launched at the same time, each plane starting to roll forward before the plane ahead of it was even in the air. Fifty-one fighter planes soared into the sky, followed by 49 high-level bombers, then 51 dive-bombers, then 40 torpedo bombers. The entire launch had taken only 15 minutes, and it was 6:15 A.M.as the 191 planes headed toward Hawaii, with a red sun rising to their left.

An Aichi D3A1 "Val"

Chapter 4

THE ATTACK ON PEARL HARBOR

The United States had developed radar by 1941, and the U.S. Army and Navy had quickly put it to use. There were radar stations in Hawaii, and one of these detected the huge flight of Japanese planes while they were still far out over the sea. But although they were reported, the army officer who should have raised an alarm did nothing. There had not been any declaration of war, so the idea of an attack didn't even occur to him. He believed that the radar blips were probably a flight of American planes.

The Zero fighters at the front of the formation began coming over the northern tip of Oahu at about 7:40 A.M. In minutes they saw Pearl Harbor ahead, with the row of American battleships clearly visible, moored close together. There was not a single American fighter plane in the sky and not a single burst of smoke from an American anti-aircraft gun. Everything looked so bright and peaceful that some of the Japanese pilots regretted that they were going to have to attack this place.

Pearl Harbor, December 7, 1941

The squadrons began to split up and head for the targets they had been assigned. The pilots all knew exactly where to go, for they had been studying maps and models of Oahu and Pearl Harbor for months.

The fighters fanned out in groups making for the army bases of Wheeler Field and Schofield Barracks, some distance inland from the harbor. Roaring low over these targets, they strafed everything in sight. They machine-gunned the planes lined up in rows, the men running for cover, the barracks where men were still sleeping, and the mess halls where they were eating breakfast. Planes burst into flames, and American soldiers and airmen died without even knowing what had hit them.

The dive-bombers broke into two groups, one heading toward the naval air base on Ford Island, in the center of Pearl Harbor, the other droning toward Wheeler Field. The torpedo bombers dropped down until they were no more than 100 feet (30 meters) or so above the water level of the harbor. The high-level bombers stayed high, circling until their turn to drop their bombs came.

Aboard the ships, heads were beginning to turn upward as the roar of plane engines grew. At first there was simply curiosity about what all these planes were doing flying over the harbor so early in the day. Curiosity turned suddenly to shock as sailors and marines saw that the wings and sides of the planes bore the round red rising-sun emblem of the Japanese Empire. The loud WHUMP of a bomb bursting on Ford Island brought the realization that this was an attack!

The torpedo planes came in low over the water and began releasing their missiles at the ships in Battleship Row. The *Nevada*, at the front of the row, was hit by a torpedo that blew a hole in her side. She was still able to move, and got under way heading for the harbor entrance with her anti-aircraft guns blazing at the enemy planes.

A Japanese bomber over Pearl Harbor

The *West Virginia* took six torpedoes. She settled into the mud on the harbor's bottom with only her superstructure above the water and burning like a forest fire. One hundred and five of her crewmen died.

Four torpedoes ripped open the *Oklahoma*'s side. Water started to pour in, and the ship began to lean to that side. The order to abandon ship was blared over the ship's loudspeakers, and men began jumping over the side. The ship rolled over and turned bottom up. Four hundred and fifteen men were killed, many of them trapped alive and drowned when the ship turned over.

The *California* took two torpedoes that caused flooding in some of her compartments, and her front end began to settle into the mud.

The ships hit by torpedoes were either by themselves or were the outer ship of a pair. The inner ships were protected from torpedoes by the ships beside them, but not from bombs dropped from above. Dive-bombers hit the *Arizona* with five bombs. One of these went into a storage area and started a fire. There was 1,600 pounds (726 kilograms) of gunpowder in the storage area, and it blew up with enough force to lift the *Arizona* out of the water and break her in two. The two parts sank down into the harbor's bottom. Over the water a cloud of black smoke was boiling into the air. About 1,100 of the *Arizona*'s crew went down with her.

The *Tennessee* was hit by two bombs that caused heavy damage, but only five crewmen were killed. The *Maryland* also took two bombs. The *Nevada*, heading toward the harbor entrance, took two bombs but managed to keep on going. Fifty of her men were killed. The *California*, already hit by two torpedoes, was hit by a bomb that exploded on her lower deck, starting fires. She lay nose down in the harbor with the part of her above water billowing out a cloud of black smoke. Her losses totaled 98 men killed. The *Pennsylvania* was hit by a bomb right in the middle of her deck, which killed 18 men.

Other ships were hit as well. The cruiser *Helena* took a torpedo, and the cruiser *Raleigh* was hit by a bomb. The destroyer *Shaw* was hit by a bomb that started a fire that spread into the ammunition-storage area. A titanic explosion blew the destroyer apart. The destroyers *Curtiss*, *Cassin*, and *Downes* were all damaged by bombs. The repair ship *Vestal* sank, damaged by bombs and ablaze from fire that had spread to her from the *Arizona*. The hull of the minesweeper *Oglala* was ruptured by a torpedo explosion, and she gradually took in so much water that she rolled over.

A Japanese bomb started a fire on the USS Shaw, *causing a fire that destroyed the ship.*

Nine Japanese dive-bombers had struck the naval airfield on Ford Island, and 33 planes, nearly half of all those on the field, were destroyed or damaged. A flight of fighters had strafed the Marine Corps airfield of Ewa and destroyed 30 planes. Bombers and fighters had hit the three U.S. Army air bases on Oahu, totally destroying 65 planes and damaging half of the 166 left. Dive-bombers also attacked the naval air station on Oahu's coast, where 36 big PBY flying boats, known as Catalinas, were kept, destroying 27 and damaging six.

The Japanese had begun their attack at 7:45, and the last planes finished their bombing runs and headed back toward their carriers at about 9:45. Behind them, Pearl Harbor lay under a cloud of black boiling smoke. Eighteen American warships had been sunk or badly damaged; 261 Army, Navy, and Marine Corps airplanes had been destroyed or damaged; more than 2,200 American servicemen were dead, more than 1,100 wounded. All this had been done by the airplanes from six Japanese aircraft carriers. Only 29 Japanese planes had been shot down, by anti-aircraft fire.

The main Japanese goal had been achieved. By sinking and disabling most of the American battleships in the harbor, they had crippled the U.S. Navy's Pacific Fleet. Japan had started the war with a tremendous victory, America with a shocking defeat!

Chapter 5

AN AIR RAID AND A CHANGE OF PLANS

With the attack on Pearl Harbor, the forces of Japan almost seemed to explode in all directions, with victorious assaults on American bases and the bases of America's allies in the Pacific. Only hours after the Pearl Harbor attack, Japanese bombers made an air raid on the important U.S. Army air base of Clark Field on the Philippine island of Luzon, destroying half of the U.S. Army's 35 B-17 bombers there, and 34 of the 92 American fighter planes. Japanese troops invaded the British colony of Malaya, in the South China Sea (now a part of the nation of Malaysia), and the British colony of Hong Kong on the southern coast of China (now part of China).

Three days later, Japanese troops began landing in the Philippines and quickly captured the American island base of Guam. That same day, Japanese bombers located the only two British battleships in the Pacific and sank them. America and its allies now had no battleships in the Pacific Ocean; the Japanese had eleven.

To make things even worse for America, on December 11 Germany and Italy, which were allied with Japan, declared war on the United States. Thus, America was now confronted with war in both the Pacific and Atlantic oceans, and the need to have strong naval forces in both places.

As the year 1942 began, the Japanese continued their conquests. On January 11, Japanese naval forces invaded the Dutch East Indies (now Indonesia) with its rich oil fields. On January 12, a Japanese army invaded the British colony of Burma (now Myanmar), lying next to the enormously important British colony of India. On January 23, other Japanese naval forces captured the important seaport of Rabaul on the large island of New Britain, which then belonged to Australia. It quickly became a major base for Japanese forces. On February 27, in a desperate attempt to halt the Japanese onslaught into the Dutch East Indies, a fleet of Dutch, British, and American cruisers and destroyers was badly defeated by a Japanese fleet of four cruisers and 13 destroyers guarding the invasion force.

The Japanese seemed invincible—unbeatable. They had gained all these victories and conquests with the loss of only 23 of their smaller warships, a few hundred planes, and a few thousand soldiers and sailors. The mood throughout the United States was one of worry and concern. On the West Coast, people were actually fearfully expecting an invasion by Japanese forces.

It seemed as if without battleships the United States was helpless, and couldn't do anything to fight back. But in warfare, it is essential to fight back and try to keep an enemy off balance. Aircraft carriers were obviously now the Navy's major weapon in the Pacific, so the Navy began to use aircraft carriers as the basis for attacks against the Japanese. In February and March, small fleets of cruisers and destroyers were built around one or two of America's four aircraft carriers in the Pacific: the *Lexington*, the *Hornet*, the *Enterprise*, and the *Yorktown*. These fleets, known as task forces, were sent out to make quick raids against several Japanese bases. Planes from the carriers sank a few small ships, shot down a few Japanese planes, and did minor damage with bombs. However, these were really only tiny "nuisance" raids that were hardly even heard of by the American people.

The USS Hornet

But then something happened that thrilled and cheered everyone throughout the United States. Japan was bombed by American planes. On April 18, 16 U.S. Army B-25 bombers had come roaring over Japan in broad daylight and unloaded bombs that damaged factories and started fires in several cities. America went wild at this news! Americans felt as if finally they had struck back at the Japanese, had paid them back a little for what they had done at Pearl Harbor.

Actually, the raid did not do much real damage. But it enraged and humiliated the Japanese, who had thought Japan would never be bombed. It also puzzled and worried Japan's military leaders. B-25 bombers were big, heavy airplanes that needed a long, flat strip of ground to take off from. The nearest

A B-25 bomber on a Tokyo bombing run takes off from the USS Hornet.

American air base was Midway Island, more than 2,000 miles (3,200 kilometers) from Japan. This seemed much too far for a B-25, which had only a 1,350-mile (2,200-kilometer) range. So where had the bombers flown from?

The fact was, they had flown from an aircraft carrier!

For months, a group of Army B-25 pilots had trained to be able to take off from a distance no longer than the flight deck of an American aircraft carrier. On April 18, the 16 big airplanes had taken off from the deck of the U. S. aircraft carrier *Hornet*, which had sailed to a point only 650 miles (1,050 kilometers) from Japan.

It was, however, a one-way flight. While the B-25's had been able to take off from a carrier deck, it was impossible for them to land on one. It had been worked out in advance that they would come down in America's ally, China, and most of them did manage to make landings there, although one landed in Russia.

Even though the air raid hadn't done much damage, it had a strong effect on Japanese war plans. With all their successes and conquests to this point, the Japanese were well ahead of the schedule they had worked out for winning the war in the Pacific. They now decided they had better do some things they hadn't thought they would be able to do until much later.

The large island of New Guinea lies just above the northern tip of Australia, and a group of islands called the Solomon Islands lies a little northeast of New Guinea. The section of ocean between Australia and New Guinea and the Solomon Islands is known as the Coral Sea. The Japanese believed they needed control of the Coral Sea. They determined to attack and capture the Australian base of Port Moresby, on the coast of New Guinea, and to invade a little island called Tulagi, in the Solomons. These could become bases for an invasion of Australia.

The other Japanese intention was to attack and capture Midway Island, which was where they believed the American bombers must have come from despite the distance. Midway had to be captured so no more bombing attacks could be made—and it could become a base for an invasion of Hawaii!

Chapter 6

OPERATION "MO"

To accomplish the invasions of Port Moresby and Tulagi, a force of 27 surface warships, seven submarines, and 41 other ships was put together and organized into groups. Two were called invasion groups; a Tulagi invasion group, consisting of a troop-transport ship carrying a force of soldiers to land on Tulagi, protected by two destroyers and other small ships; and a Port Moresby invasion group: consisting of five troop transports with soldiers, protected by a cruiser, six destroyers, and some other small ships. These would be further protected by a covering group of four cruisers and a small aircraft carrier with 21 planes, a support group of two cruisers, a seaplane carrier with 13 planes, and some small ships, and a carrier group of two big carriers with a total of 125 planes, two cruisers, and six destroyers. The Japanese commanders believed all this would be enough.

The basic Japanese plan was to send all their groups into the Coral Sea, where the Tulagi Group would turn eastward to the Solomons, and the Port Moresby Group would swing west toward New Guinea. This plan was given the name Operation "MO."

Admiral Chester William Nimitz

A Douglas SBD "Dauntless" on the flight deck of the USS Yorktown. *Note the damage to the tail.*

However, Operation "MO," like most battle plans created by the Japanese naval commanders, was rather complicated. Everything really depended on each group of ships following a careful schedule with no slipups, which is often not possible in warfare. And because the Japanese knew the Americans had no battleships, and believed they had only one aircraft carrier in the Pacific, the plan also assumed the Americans would offer little opposition—which is never a good assumption to make about an enemy in warfare.

What the Japanese didn't know was that American code experts had figured out the code the Japanese used when they sent orders by radio. By mid-April, the code-breakers had learned almost everything about Operation "MO." The commander of naval forces in the Pacific, Admiral Chester Nimitz, began putting together a fleet to meet the Japanese force when it entered the Coral Sea.

The fleet was formed from three task forces that had been operating in different parts of the Pacific. One of these, Task Force 11, consisted of the aircraft carrier *Lexington*, two cruisers, and five destroyers. Another, Task Force 44, was composed of an Australian heavy and light cruiser, and an American cruiser and two destroyers. The third, Task Force 17, contained the carrier *Yorktown*, three cruisers, and four destroyers. Two oilers, and two destroyers to protect them, were added to provide the fuel for the ships of the fleet. Thus, the American force had 23 surface warships to the Japanese 27, and about 140 carrier planes to the Japanese 159.

The American fleet was put under the command of Rear Admiral Frank Jack Fletcher, who was also the commander of Task Force 17. The ships of the three task forces were shuffled about to form an Attack Group, a Support Group, and a Carrier Group. At 6:15 on the morning of May 1, the three forces came together in the Coral Sea. Admiral Fletcher immediately ordered all of them to refuel from the two oilers, the *Neosho* and *Tippecanoe*. This was a long process that continued well into the next day. At 6:00 A.M., Fletcher took his task force westward to look for the enemy, ordering the other two forces to join him as soon as they completed refueling.

The Japanese were also on the move. By May 3 at 8:00 A.M., the Tulagi Invasion Group had reached the island, and troops had begun to land. Admiral Fletcher soon received a report of this, and by 8:30 his task force was heading for Tulagi. Around sunrise on May 4, Fletcher was in position about 100 miles (160 kilometers) from Tulagi. At 6:30 in the morning, he ordered the *Yorktown* to launch a raid against the Japanese forces on the island.

American carriers had four kinds of airplanes. Like the Japanese navy, the U.S. Navy used the same kind of plane for both torpedo bombing and high-level bombing. This was the Douglas TBD "Devastator," which could carry either a 1,000-pound (454-kilogram) bomb or a 21-inch (53-centimeter) torpedo.

A Douglas TBD "Devastator"

A Grumman F4F "Wildcat"

U.S. carriers also had one kind of fighter plane; the Grumman F4F "Wildcat," with six machine guns. But the U.S. Navy used two kinds of dive-bombers. The Douglas SBD "Dauntless" carried a 500-pound (227-kilogram) bomb and was known as a scout bomber; the Douglas BD, with a 1,000-pound bomb, was classified as a "heavy" dive-bomber.

Twelve torpedo bombers and 28 dive-bombers took off and made the first attack on Tulagi. They sank a minesweeper and damaged a Japanese destroyer, which later sank. At 10:30 another raid was made by 11 torpedo bombers and 27 dive-bombers, which destroyed two seaplanes. More raids that afternoon sank four landing barges and destroyed three more seaplanes. Actually, these were not very effective raids. However, a rumor swept throughout the task force that the Japanese force had been nearly wiped out!

By seven o'clock the next morning, the Japanese carrier group was entering the Coral Sea. At a little after eight o'clock, the three American task forces came together and began to head northwest. The two opposing carrier forces were now heading directly toward each other without knowing it.

By now the oiler *Neosho* was empty, and on the evening of May 6, the *Neosho* and its guardian destroyer the *Sims* were detached from the American force to proceed back to Pearl Harbor. This was to be a significant event.

The USS Lexington

Early the next morning, Admiral Fletcher received a report that a group of Japanese ships had been sighted heading for Port Moresby. This was undoubtedly the Port Moresby invasion group. Fletcher had to try to stop it; that was why he was in the Coral Sea. But he didn't want to send out any of his airplanes, because he was expecting to have to fight the Japanese aircraft-carrier group at any moment. Instead, he decided to send his support group, formed of two Australian cruisers and an American cruiser and two destroyers, commanded by British Rear Admiral J. G. Crace. Fletcher was sure that Crace's ships could easily deal with the cruiser and six destroyers protecting the invasion force, and could then destroy the troop ships and end the threat to Port Moresby. At 6:45, he sent Crace to find the invasion force and attack it. Then he ordered a number of planes launched to search for the Japanese carriers.

At almost the same time, Rear Admiral Tadaichi Hara, in charge of the Japanese carrier force, was acting along the same line. Search planes went out looking for American ships. At 7:36, a Japanese pilot spotted the American oiler *Neosho* and destroyer *Sims* all by themselves. He mistook them for a carrier and cruiser, and reported them as such. Thinking he had an American carrier at his mercy, Admiral Hara immediately ordered an all-out attack by dive-bombers and torpedo planes from his carriers *Zuikaku* and *Shokaku*.

Only a short time after that, Fletcher's scout planes also spotted something. At 8:15, a pilot radioed a report back to the *Yorktown* that he had seen two Japanese carriers and four cruisers.

This was what Admiral Fletcher had been waiting for. He ordered a massive air strike. The *Lexington* began launching planes at 9:26, the *Yorktown* at about 10:00. By 10:30, 93 American planes were heading toward the area where the Japanese carriers had been reported.

Chapter 7

THE BATTLE OF THE CORAL SEA

Actually, this attack was a serious mistake. What the scout planes had really seen was not the Japanese carrier group but the support group—two light cruisers, three little vessels known as gunboats, and a seaplane carrier with 13 planes used mainly for scouting. Thus, Fletcher's all-out air strike was being sent against a target that really didn't mean much, and it was leaving his two carriers virtually unprotected against an air strike by planes from the Japanese carrier group now heading toward them.

But luck was going to be on Fletcher's side. At a little after eleven o'clock on May 7, the planes from the *Lexington* were near the point where their target was supposed to be. The pilot at the head of the flight began peering about at the vast blue surface beneath him for some sign of the enemy ships. Suddenly, he caught sight of a cluster of what looked like white threads lying on the deep blue. He knew these were the wakes of ships—the long trails of foamy white that a ship leaves behind it as it slices through the water. In moments, the entire flight was heading after the wakes, and soon, a group of ships was sighted.

By sheer luck this was not the little support group, it was the Japanese covering group, which included the light aircraft carrier *Shoho*, with 21 planes. Even at that moment, the *Shoho* was readying an air strike against the two American carriers, but now its chance was over. The American planes streaked toward it. The war's first American air attack on an enemy aircraft carrier was about to begin!

The *Shoho* had been caught by surprise, with numerous planes sitting on its flight deck and one coming up on the elevator. The carrier quickly turned into the wind, in a desperate attempt to begin launching as many planes as it could. The Japanese fighter planes above it raced toward the Americans, and every ship around the carrier opened up with its anti-aircraft guns, filling the sky with black puffs of exploding shells.

The fighter planes of the *Lexington* flight headed for the oncoming Japanese fighters; the *Lexington* dive-bombers sped through the black puffs and began to "peel off," one after another, in dives heading almost straight down at *Shoho*. First in line was the commander of the scout-bomber squadron, Lieutenant Commander Robert Dixon. His 500-pound (227-kilogram) bomb hit squarely in the middle of the carrier's wooden flight deck, demolishing it and scattering airplanes about. This damage would keep the *Shoho* from being able to launch any of its planes.

The second plane's bomb missed the ship but exploded in the water, close enough so that two Japanese planes were thrown off the deck into the sea. The third plane's bomb made a direct hit on a group of anti-aircraft guns on one side of the ship, destroying them all.

The fourth and fifth planes were fighting off Japanese Zeros all the way down, but still managed to drop their bombs. One was a miss, one a hit.

Now the attack of the "heavy" dive-bomber squadron began. The 1,000-pound bombs these planes carried could do a

During the Battle of the Coral Sea, an unidentified Japanese carrier, probably the Shoho, *makes a sharp evasive maneuver.*

great deal more damage than the 500-pound bombs of the "light" scout bombers. The first pilot's bomb struck the flight deck with a tremendous fiery explosion. Most of the bombs of the following planes also hit the target. The entire deck of the *Shoho* became a sea of flame.

In the meantime, the *Lexington*'s torpedo bombers were making their attack. They used the smoke from *Shoho*'s fire, rolling out over the sea, to hide their approach from any Japanese fighter planes that might be overhead. This enabled them to get in very close. One after another they launched their torpedoes and veered away, and one after another, twelve torpedoes slammed into the side of the Japanese carrier, literally ripping her wide open!

The *Shoho* was a mangled wreck, burning fiercely and drifting helplessly with no power. She was finished. Her commanding officer ordered all surviving crewmen to abandon ship. At about 11:35, the *Shoho* slipped beneath the water and vanished.

Back in the radio room of the *Lexington,* off-duty officers and others were tuned to the frequency that carried the reports of the pilots making the attack. Suddenly, they heard the exultant voice of Lieutenant Commander Dixon. "Scratch one flat-top!" he declared. "Dixon to carrier—scratch one flat-top!" What this meant in naval terms was that one aircraft carrier—a "flat-top"—had been "scratched"—wiped out, like a name on a list being scratched out by the stroke of a pen.

The second piece of luck for Admiral Fletcher took place about noon. The Japanese dive-bombers from the *Shokaku* and *Zuikaku* that had been sent out to go after the American "carrier" and "cruiser" that had supposedly been sighted, found the *Neosho* and *Sims*. About 16 of the planes went after the *Sims*; the other 20 roared toward the *Neosho*. The destroyer began taking defensive action, zigzagging sharply and firing all her anti-aircraft guns, knocking down one Japanese plane. But she was hit by three 500-pound bombs and began to sink within minutes. Most of the more than 250 men of her crew perished.

The *Neosho* couldn't even try to defend herself. Seven bombs slammed into her, and one Japanese pilot deliberately crashed his plane onto her deck. Flaming gasoline gushed out of the plane's broken tanks and started fires. Men of the *Neosho*'s crew began jumping into the water.

However, the *Neosho* continued to float for several days. She was found by an American destroyer, which rescued the 123 men left out of the crew of 258. Four other survivors, on a life raft, were also rescued later.

Dreadful though the loss of so many men was, the attacks on the *Sims* and *Neosho* may well have served to save the lives of hundreds of other men of the American fleet, as well as other ships. For by going after the oiler and destroyer under the impression they were a carrier and cruiser, the Japanese pilots had missed a chance to catch the real carriers, the *Lexington* and *Yorktown*, unprotected while most of their planes were out attacking the *Shoho*. If those two carriers had both been sunk, America might have had to stop fighting and seek peace!

While all these air attacks were going on, Admiral Crace's force was continuing to race toward the point at which he hoped to catch the Port Moresby invasion group. Crace didn't know that the invasion group had been called back. Admiral Inouye, in charge of the entire Japanese invasion operation, had come down with a case of "jitters," and decided to hold up on the invasion until he knew for sure where all the American ships were.

At just about two o'clock in the afternoon, Crace's ships came under attack by eleven Japanese bombers that had been sent out from Rabaul. Crace's diamond formation of ships sent up such a curtain of anti-aircraft fire that it drove these planes off. Soon after, another group of 12 bombers attacked. Crace's ships shot down five of them, and the rest hurriedly departed. Then 19 high-flying bombers appeared, but every one of their bombs missed. Crace kept on going.

By about 1:40 P.M. all but three of the American planes from the *Lexington* and *Yorktown* were safely back to their carriers. By 3:50 P.M., both the *Lexington* and *Yorktown* were ready to launch again.

Admiral Fletcher decided against it, however. He didn't know where the two big Japanese carriers were, but he was pretty sure they knew where *his* carriers were. He decided to keep his planes ready for any attack they might send against him.

As darkness fell, Fletcher thought about sending planes out to make a night attack, but decided not to do it. At almost the same time, both Admiral Inouye, in Rabaul, and Admiral Takagi, in command of the Japanese carrier group, were also thinking about night attacks. They, too, decided against it. The night passed quietly.

Chapter 8

A BATTLE OF CARRIERS

May 8 dawned. At 6:25, Admiral Fletcher sent out planes from the *Lexington* to make a sweep search about 200 miles (320 kilometers) wide around his ships. At 8:38 one of the planes spotted the entire Japanese carrier group and radioed back its course and speed. Fletcher immediately ordered a full air strike from both the *Lexington* and *Yorktown*. By 9:15 the *Lexington* had launched 41 planes, by 9:25 the *Yorktown* had sent up 43. The 84 planes sped toward the position of the Japanese carriers.

A little before 11:00, the *Yorktown*'s planes sighted the Japanese ships. The carriers saw them coming, and the *Shokaku* turned into the wind and began launching fighters while the *Zuikaku* quickly headed into a heavy rain squall with thick clouds overhead, and became lost to sight.

With only the *Shokaku* in view, the *Yorktown*'s torpedo bombers headed straight for it. However, they ran into a storm of anti-aircraft fire from both the carrier and the cruisers and destroyers guarding it, and had to launch their torpedoes at a considerable distance from the carrier.

This revealed a dreadful problem. The American pilots discovered that at long range their torpedoes were simply no good! The torpedo attacks against the carrier *Shoho* had been successful because the planes had been able to get very close, but now the pilots found that when they had to drop their torpedoes at a great distance, the missiles traveled so slowly that a Japanese ship could easily turn aside and let them go by. Worse still, the few torpedoes that did hit didn't explode! The entire torpedo-bomber attack was a dismal failure.

The *Yorktown* dive-bombers did a little better. Two of their bombs scored hits that started fires and damaged the *Shokaku*'s flight deck so badly that no more planes could be launched from the carrier.

At about 11:40, planes from the *Lexington* arrived. But they were only the torpedo bomber squadron, for the dive-bomber squadron had run into a rainy overcast that hid the ocean beneath them, and they finally headed back to their carrier. The torpedo bombers attacked at once, but made the same discovery the *Yorktown* torpedo planes had—their torpedoes were worthless at long range. They, too, failed to make any hits.

Thus, the *Shokaku* was not badly hurt. However, she could no longer launch any aircraft and was useless for any further offensive action and unable to defend herself. Most of her planes were taken aboard the *Zuikaku,* and she turned away and headed toward home, where she would spend months being repaired.

Meanwhile, the *Lexington*'s radar was showing numerous blips about 70 miles (110 kilometers) away and heading straight toward it. Before the *Shokaku* and *Zuikaku* had been attacked, they had launched 70 planes to go after the American carriers, and now those planes had arrived! The *Lexington*'s air-raid siren went on—and immediately jammed, keeping up a steady howl that continued throughout the entire raid that followed.

Torpedo planes came in first, in two waves: the first wave low over the water, the second wave high, both heading for the *Lexington*'s port side. At about 2,400 feet (720 meters) from the ship, they dropped their torpedoes. The Japanese torpedoes were better than the American ones. The *Lexington* shuddered as a torpedo struck, and shuddered again as she was hit once more.

To make matters worse, the dive-bombers were also now making their attack. Two bombs hit the *Lexington*'s deck, one wiping out three anti-aircraft guns and starting a fire, another hitting the smokestacks. Then another torpedo slammed into the carrier's side!

The *Yorktown* was also under attack. A 1,000-pound bomb from a dive-bomber tore through her flight deck and exploded on the fourth deck, killing 66 men and starting a fire.

The attack was over by 11:45. The *Yorktown* was in fairly good shape, ready to launch more planes and keep fighting if necessary. The *Lexington* was tilting steeply to one side, with fires burning, three boiler rooms flooded, and the elevator that lifted planes to the flight deck unable to operate. But she was still afloat and looked as if she could make it to home port, where she could be repaired and go out to fight again. At this point, the American fleet seemed to be the clear victor in the battle, having lost only an oiler and a destroyer, while the Japanese had suffered the loss of a carrier and a number of smaller ships.

However, one of the torpedo hits on the *Lexington* had damaged a gasoline tank, and fumes were leaking from it. They reached an electrical generator that had been left running and was shooting off sparks. There was a titanic explosion that shook the entire ship. More explosions followed, fires spread. It was soon obvious that here was no chance to save the carrier. By 5:30 that evening, rafts were cast loose and the crew began to abandon ship.

At 8:00, Admiral Fletcher ordered the destroyer *Phelps* to torpedo the *Lexington* and sink her so that she couldn't fall into enemy hands. This was done, and the "Lady Lex," as she was known throughout the navy, sank into the sea. From the other ships they had been taken to, the men who had served aboard the *Lexington* watched with tears streaming down their faces.

That night, having received an order from Admiral Nimitz to withdraw from the Coral Sea and return to Hawaii, the American ships turned and began sailing southward. Admiral Crace's little group of Australian and American ships returned to Australia.

The Japanese pilots that had attacked the two American carriers returned to their own fleet, and reported that they had sunk both. When Admiral Inouye read their reports, he believed that the American fleet was finished. However, he

The crew of the USS Lexington *abandons ship.*

decided not to risk making the Port Moresby invasion, because without the *Shoho* and *Shokaku* to help provide air cover, the troop transports would be in serious danger from U.S. Army bombers flying out of Australia. He, too, ordered all his forces to leave the Coral Sea and return to Rabaul.

The Battle of the Coral Sea was over. The Japanese had lost 43 planes, one light carrier, one destroyer, and several minesweepers, and had one big carrier badly damaged and put out of action for a long time. The Americans had lost 33 planes, one big carrier, a destroyer, and an oiler, and had their other carrier damaged but not put out of action. But the important thing was that the Japanese had been forced to turn back and give up on their attempt to capture Port Moresby. Admiral Fletcher had done what he had been sent to do—prevent the Japanese invasion and capture of Port Moresby. It was an American victory, the first victory in the five months since Pearl Harbor!

The Battle of the Coral Sea was the world's first sea battle fought entirely between aircraft carriers. The cruisers and destroyers never even came in sight of any enemy ship and never even fired any of their big guns.

Chapter 9

AIRCRAFT CARRIERS— THE NEW RULERS OF THE SEA

On June 3, only 27 days after the Battle of the Coral Sea, American and Japanese forces met head-on once again. The Japanese tried to carry out their plan for capturing the American base at Midway, and an American fleet was there to stop them. The Battle of Midway, like the Battle of the Coral Sea, was fought mainly by carriers and their airplanes, with battleships, cruisers, and destroyers never even coming in sight of one another. Aircraft carriers had become the major, decisive weapon in naval battles!

The Japanese Midway fleet was in three groups under the command of Admiral Yamamoto. One group consisted of the four big carriers with a few battleships, cruisers, and destroyers; a second group had seven battleships, a small carrier with only eight planes, and some cruisers and destroyers; the third group was the invasion force of 11 troop ships carrying 5,000 soldiers, guarded by some battleships, cruisers, destroyers, and the other small carrier.

The American battle fleet was formed of Task Force 17, made up of the *Yorktown*, two cruisers, and six destroyers, and

Planes from the USS Hornet *bomb a Japanese cruiser at the Battle of Midway.*

commanded by Admiral Fletcher, and Task Force 16, composed of the carriers *Hornet* and *Enterprise*, six cruisers, nine destroyers, and two tankers. It was commanded by Admiral Raymond Spruance. Fletcher was in command of the entire fleet.

The battle began with the four Japanese carriers sending an air raid against Midway, to "soften it up" so that Japanese troops could easily land. But meanwhile, the American carriers launched a massive air strike against the Japanese carrier force.

At first, everything went against the Americans. Scores of their torpedo bombers were shot down by Japanese Zekes and anti-aircraft fire. Not a single American torpedo did any damage to an enemy carrier.

But suddenly, American dive-bomber squadrons appeared high overhead. And in a tremendous stroke of luck, there was not a single Japanese fighter plane able to attack them—the fighters were all down low, where they had gone to attack the torpedo planes. The bombers nosed over into screaming dives, each squadron picking out a carrier.

Four bombs hit the *Kaga*, demolishing the superstructure and setting the entire flight deck aflame. Two bombs struck the *Akagi*, one tearing through the flight deck and exploding on the hangar deck, setting it afire, the other starting a fire on the flight deck. One bomb set the *Soryu*'s hangar deck on fire, two others pulverized the flight deck. In only a few minutes, three Japanese carriers had become mangled, burning, sinking wrecks. The battle had turned entirely in America's favor!

But the Japanese carrier *Hiryu*, which had not been hit, now launched all her available planes. They found the *Yorktown*.

Eighteen dive-bombers roared toward it. Ten were shot down, but eight got through. Three bombs hit the carrier, putting a hole in the flight deck and starting fires.

The *Yorktown*'s crew put out the fires and repaired the flight deck. But then, more of the *Hiryu*'s planes arrived—ten torpedo bombers. Six were shot down, but four managed to launch their torpedoes. Two hit, putting a hole in the *Yorktown*'s hull and damaging the rudder so it couldn't steer.

However, American scout planes had now located the *Hiryu*, and an air attack was immediately launched from the *Enterprise* and *Hornet*. Dive-bombers streaked toward the Japanese carrier and attacked. A bomb set the hangar deck aflame, two others destroyed the flight deck. The *Hiryu* was left burning, drifting, and helpless.

The USS Yorktown *is badly damaged during the Battle of Midway.*

The next day, a Japanese submarine located the *Yorktown*, being towed to safety, and slammed torpedoes into it and the destroyer with it. The destroyer sank at once, the *Yorktown* began to sink slowly. Later in the day, American dive-bombers found a Japanese cruiser lagging behind the Japanese fleet and sank it.

That ended the battle. The Americans had lost a carrier and a destroyer. The Japanese had lost four carriers and a cruiser. The Japanese fleet pulled back and left, giving up on the plan to capture Midway.

The Battle of Midway was a tremendous victory for the United States, and it actually turned the whole war in America's favor. The loss of four carriers put the Japanese at such a disadvantage that from then on they were never able to attempt to capture enemy bases nor continue their conquests. Now it was the United States that went on the offensive, as American marines and soldiers began invading one Japanese base after another, and capturing them.

But the clash of carrier versus carrier on the sea was not yet finished. On June 19, 1944, the biggest carrier battle of the entire war began, involving 24 carriers from both sides, the Battle of the Philippine Sea. A Japanese force of five big carriers, including two newly built ones, four small carriers, five battleships, 13 cruisers, and 28 destroyers sailed toward the island of Saipan, in the western Pacific, to try to prevent an American invasion. Most of the American fleet was gathered there, and if the Japanese could catch it by surprise, they might score a tremendous victory.

However, the Japanese were still not aware that the United States had deciphered their codes. The American naval commanders knew the Japanese were coming, and the American fleet was lying in wait. It consisted of seven big carriers, eight small ones, seven battleships, 21 cruisers, 69 destroyers, and a number of submarines. This time, the Japanese were going to be outnumbered!

At one minute before ten o'clock in the morning, American radar screens indicated a large flight of planes approaching from the west. Vice Admiral Marc Mitscher, commanding the American carrier force, knew this was the first wave of Japanese attacks. He instantly ordered up fighter squadrons from the carriers *Bunker Hill, Cowpens, Essex,* and *Princeton.*

They ran into a flight of 69 dive-bombers and torpedo bombers. This was the beginning of one of the most one-sided air battles of the war. Japan had lost its best, most skillful pilots at the Coral Sea and Midway, and Japanese carrier planes were now being flown by poorly trained, inexperienced men who were no match for the experienced American pilots. The Americans shot down 45 of the 69 first-wave attackers. During the rest of the day, Americans shot down 171 of 212 Japanese planes that tried attacking the American carriers!

American submarines had been very busy, too. One slammed torpedoes into the big Japanese carrier *Shokaku,* and sent her to the bottom. Another torpedoed the newly built *Taiho,* biggest of all the Japanese carriers, and she sank instantly.

At 3:40 the next afternoon, American search planes found the Japanese fleet and reported its position. At once, Admiral Mitscher ordered up a full air strike of 216 dive-bombers and torpedo planes. At about 6:40 they located their target and went to work. Two torpedoes hit the carrier *Hiyo,* and it started to sink. The carrier *Zuikaku* was hit and damaged. Two tankers were damaged. Then it became too dark for the raid to continue, and the Americans turned away.

That ended the Battle of the Philippine Sea. The Japanese force slipped away during the night, with three of its five big carriers gone and only 35 of the 473 planes it started out with left! The American fleet had one carrier damaged and 130 planes lost out of 956.

Aircraft carriers also played a big part in the last and biggest naval battle of the war, the Battle of Leyte Gulf. In October

A Japanese carrier under attack from U.S. planes during the Battle of Leyte Gulf

1944, American forces began the invasion to recapture the Philippines. The Japanese Navy combined just about every ship it had left into a force to try to prevent the invasion. For three days, 282 ships of both sides dodged and pursued and fought; hundreds and hundreds of planes filled the air. The Japanese superbattleship *Musashi* was sunk by American carrier planes, which also sank all four of Japan's last big carriers. By the end of the battle, the Japanese fleet had virtually been destroyed.

Aircraft carriers played a major part in the war between America and Japan. The weapon that had started the war as an "eggshell" for assisting or defending battleships had become the main weapon of the navy. Sea warfare had changed forever. Today, battleships exist only as floating museums. Carriers are now the most important kind of ship for a navy—the ships around which the task forces of today are built.

Index